CONTENTS

From unscrambled words write the correct name of each object.

bta   Bat

llba

nat

gba 

hoes

rdbi

npe
Kobo
gmu

Singing

Dancing

Running

Writing

Laughing

Reading

Bathing

Cooking

Swimming

Tick the correct picture whose name begins with letter 'B'

Match the half part to make it full

Write the missing alphabets
A
F
H

U
X
Z

Write the missing numbers in reverse order from (30—1)

30			
	25		
			21

COUNT AND COLOR THE ANIMALS

TOTAL

PAGE:20
TOTAL

TOTAL

Help the animals to reach their home

Help puppy to reach it's kennel by writing missing numbers.

Help the lion to reach it's den by writing the missing numbers

Den

8 [ ] 10

5

3 [ ] 1

Help the bird to reach it's nest by counting.

Put '>,'<or=signs in the blanks:-

1. 15 < 20

2. 76 ☐ 50

3. 37 ☐ 37

4. 0   10

5. 100 > 75

6. 50   50

7. Rs 60 ☐ Rs 90

8. $5 ☐ $9

9. £7 ☐ £3

Mathematics puzzles

IF, = 5
AND = 2
THEN,
+ - = 8
+ + + =
- =

$$5 \times 3 = 15$$

$$16 \div 2 = 8$$

$$100 - \square = 20$$

Put circle on the correct answer

A bull has **1,5,3(2)** horns.

A dear has **5, 4, 3, 2** legs.

A spider has 8,6,4,5 legs.

Which one runs fast:-

Which one is autotrophs :-

Which one has wheels?

Which one is bigger?

Count all the books given.

Total =

Count all the red
books from the
given books

Total =

Count all the Yellow and green books

Total green

Total red

Name the colors:-

= Violet

=

Fill the blanks using 'Gr'or ' go:-'

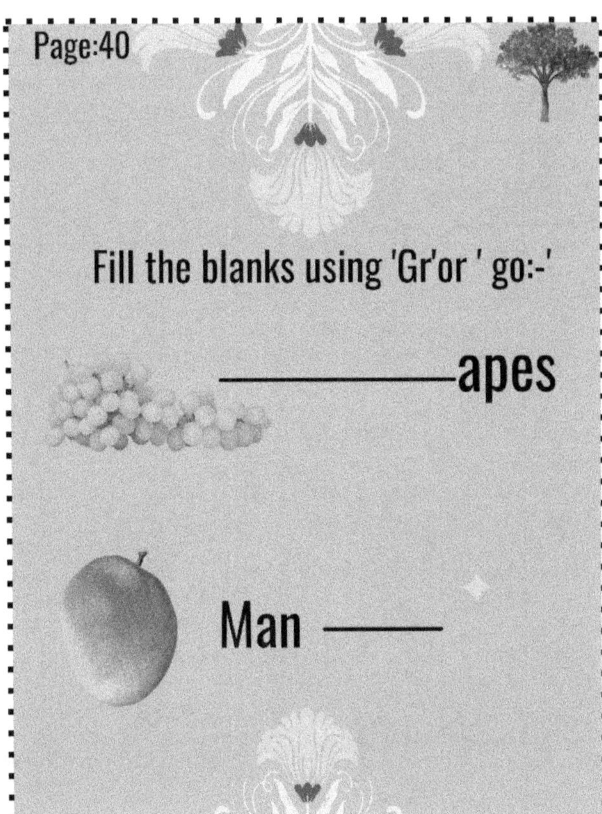

——————apes

Man ———

Fill the blanks using 'ON 'or ' ROT:-'

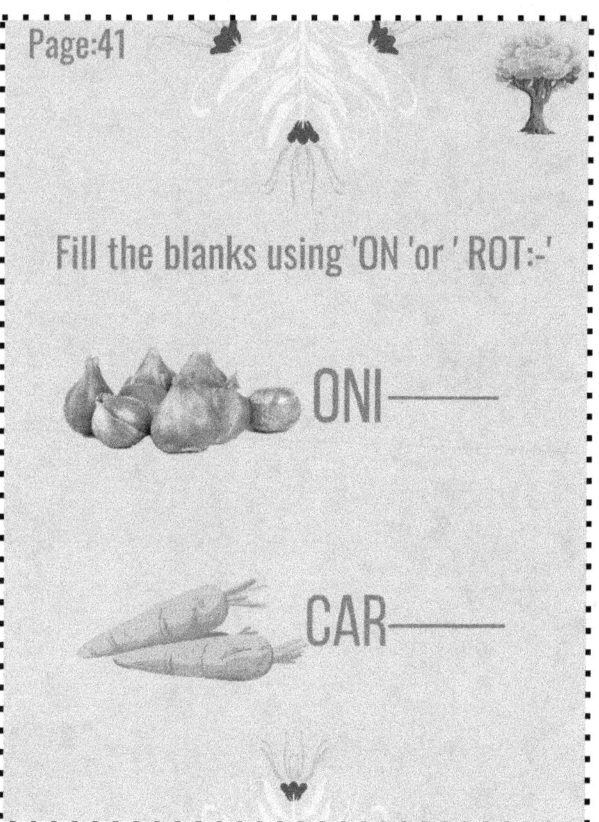

ONI———

CAR———

Fill the blanks using 'LEO 'or ' HO:-'

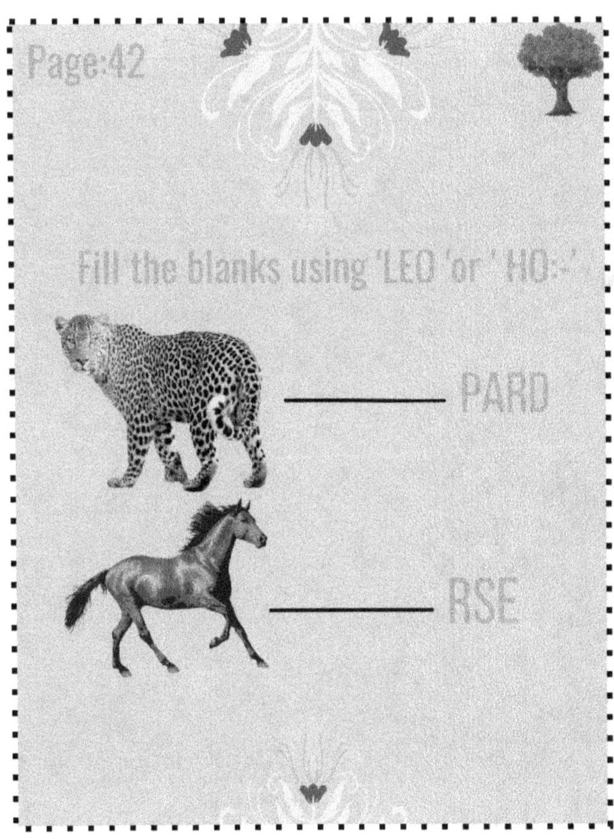

——————— PARD

——————— RSE

Match the correct shadows of the given objects